Voices

an imprint of dalmatian publishing group

VOICES:

REFLECTIONS ON AN AMERICAN ICON THROUGH WORDS AND SONG

Published by Dalmatian Press, an imprint of Dalmatian Publishing Group.
Copyright © 2007 by Dalmatian Publishing Group, LLC
All rights reserved (Printed in China)

The DALMATIAN PRESS name and logo are trademarks of
Dalmatian Publishing Group, Atlanta, Georgia 30329.

All photographs are © **AP Images** with the following exceptions
© Flip Schulke/CORBIS: cover
© AP Images/Gene Herrick: p. 17
© AP Images/Bill Hudson: p. 26
© AP Images/JAB: p. 50
© AP Images/Horace Court: p. 54
© AP Images/Jack Thornell: p. 60
© AP Images/Charles Kelly: p. 65
© AP Images/FAW: p. 69
© AP Images/RJ: p. 70
© AP Images/Charles Dharapak: p. 82
© AP Images/Dave Martin: p. 85
© Brent Cook: pp. 73, 75, 86

ISBN: 1-40374-238-3
16740-0807

07 08 09 10 GSP 10 9 8 7 6 5 4 3 2 1

You always need music.
You need the Negro spirituals.
I think music lifts our spirits and informs us,
and that's the job of music.
And if you go back to the enslaved Africans:
If they hadn't had a song,
how would they have remained sane?
They created this body of work that
has become the voice of America.
From the spirituals, we flow into gospel, jazz, blues ...
that's how you pass the story along.

—NIKKI GIOVANNI

introduction

VOICES WAS ENVISIONED AS a tribute to the life of Martin Luther King, Jr., and inspired by the music of the Civil Rights movement—music that Dr. King loved so much.

King, in fact, considered music to be the soul of the movement. Folk songs, spirituals, and hymns heartened protesters as they stood up to fire hoses, dog attacks, and arrests. And one song, *We Shall Overcome*, became the movement's anthem.

"The freedom songs are playing a strong and vital role in our struggle," King once said. "They give people new courage and a sense of unity. I think they keep alive a faith, a radiant hope in the future, particularly in our most trying times."

Civil Rights activists sang through humiliation and intimidation. They blended their voices on lengthy freedom marches, and harmonized in jail, for strength, inspiration, and solace. Music embraced them all, in companionship and a common cause. The CD accompanying *Voices* was compiled from performances presented by The Choral Arts Society of Washington. Some songs were especially dear to Dr. King and remind us "that we are all brothers and sisters," says Society Artistic Director Norman Scribner.

Voices: Reflections on an American Icon Through Words and Song is divided into five sections that resound with this musical theme and follow the history of King's Civil Rights work: Discord, Crescendo, March Toward Harmony, Elegy, and Symphony. These sections complement the CD and offer hope that King's work will continue to inspire the world to create what he called a "symphony of brotherhood."

The book's quotes and anecdotes attest to King's legacy in the public consciousness 40 years after his death. They include the reflections of everyday observers, children, and adults from different walks of life.

Some remembrances were gathered from foot soldiers who marched with Dr. King. Others come from distinguished witnesses to history, such as former Georgia legislator Julian Bond, U.S. Rep. John Lewis, and Harris Wofford, assistant to President John F. Kennedy—as well as prominent writers, like the spirited poet Nikki Giovanni, Pulitzer Prize-winner Gene Patterson, and journalist John Seigenthaler, an assistant to Attorney General Robert F. Kennedy.

Nobel Peace Prize-winner Jimmy Carter and other U.S. Presidents offer thoughts on King and the Civil Rights movement, along with Archbishop Desmond Tutu, Dorothy Height, Chair Emerita of the National Council of Negro Women, and Marian Wright Edelman, who speaks for the children of the world as President of the Children's Defense Fund.

Many people moved by the Civil Rights crusade admired Dr. King; some, both black and white, opposed him. And others seemed unaware of his charismatic presence. Still, America was transformed by King's leadership, and his vision.

The voice of Martin Luther King, Jr., was stilled in 1968, but his message reverberates today, and the sounds of the Civil Rights movement linger on.

We Shall Overcome

We shall overcome
We shall overcome
We shall overcome some day

Oh, deep in my heart
I do believe
We shall overcome some day

We'll walk hand in hand
We'll walk hand in hand
We'll walk hand in hand some day

Oh, deep in my heart
I do believe
We shall overcome some day

We shall all be free
We shall all be free
We shall all be free some day

Oh, deep in my heart
I do believe
We shall overcome some day

(Traditional)

discord

1954–1959

*I have come to the conclusion
that the ultimate measure of a man is not
where he finds himself in moments of
COMFORT and moments of
CONVENIENCE, but where he finds
himself in moments of CHALLENGE
and moments of CONTROVERSY.*

Martin Luther King, Jr.

IN THE 1950S, long after Lincoln signed the Emancipation Proclamation and smoke had cleared from the Civil War, the American South remained segregated. Many hotels, restaurants, and theaters were closed to blacks; public facilities, such as schools, were considered "separate but equal"; and bathrooms and water fountains were labeled "Colored" or "White." Access to the voting booth was limited, and mothers of black children cautioned youngsters to mind their manners with whites.

Then on May 17, 1954, the Supreme Court made a landmark decision calling for the desegregation of American schools. The next year, a 14-year-old black boy from Chicago named Emmett Till was brutally murdered in Mississippi, and three months later, Rosa Parks, a black seamstress, was arrested in Montgomery, Alabama, for refusing to give up—to a white man—her seat on the bus.

This simple act of civil disobedience mobilized the black community. And a young minister from Georgia, fresh out of divinity school and new to the pulpit of the Dexter Avenue Baptist Church, felt called to lead his people in the quest for freedom.

Martin Luther King, Jr., who had a profound respect for Mahatma Gandhi's success in leading India to independence, decided to use Gandhi's emphasis on nonviolence as his model for social reform.

Violence, King said, only added darkness "to a night already devoid of stars." Only love could drive out hate.

September 1954

September 1954 — After completing work on his doctorate in systematic theology at Boston University, King is named pastor of Dexter Avenue Baptist Church in Montgomery, Alabama.

discord

I had felt for a long time that if I was ever told to get up
so a white person could sit, that I would refuse to do so.

—ROSA PARKS

When something happened to the Negroes in
the South, I said, "That's their business, not mine."
Now I know how wrong I was. The murder of my
son has shown me that what happens to any of us
anywhere in the world had better be the business of us all.

—MAMIE TILL-MOBLEY

December 5, 1955 — King is elected president of the Montgomery Improvement Association after seamstress Rosa Parks is arrested for refusing to give up her seat on a bus to a white man. The association orchestrates a boycott of the bus system that lasts 382 days.

discord

As a young child, I had tasted the bitter fruits of segregation and racism,
and I didn't like it. I would ask my mother and ask my father,
my grandparents and great-grandparents,
"Why segregation? Why racial discrimination?" And they would say,
"That's the way it is. Don't get in trouble. Don't get in the way."
Martin Luther King, Jr., inspired me and thousands of other Americans
to get in the way. He inspired us to get in trouble.
But it was good trouble; it was necessary trouble.

—U.S. REP. JOHN LEWIS, D-GA

Dr. King's moral vision was such that throughout his career he was told
it was "too early" for the reform he was advocating at any given time.
Yet at the crucial points of his career—Montgomery, Birmingham, Selma—
he was always right in determining a "state of readiness" for change existed
where it was invisible to other eyes. Certainly, in 1955, no one would have
predicted that Montgomery's black population would be bold enough to
protest bus segregation in one of the citadels of segregationist thought.

—HOWELL RAINES

November 13, 1956 — The U.S. Supreme Court
rules that public bus segregation is illegal.

discord

*When I first met Martin Luther King, he was 15 years
old and he had come to Morehouse as a gifted student.
Even then he was trying to make a decision about
whether he would go into medicine or law or the
ministry, and he was very serious about it, his dream.
I say to young people, he was not assassinated because
he had a dream. It was because he dreamed of ways to
change the system and he had a vision of what America
could be and he worked at that. More and more young
people, as they understand that a little bit deeper, need
to think, "What is it now that I should be doing?"*

—DOROTHY HEIGHT

*It is not often that great leaders and great turning points
in history converge and sweep us up in a movement.
My generation was blessed beyond measure
to be in the right place at the right time
to experience and help bring transforming changes
to the South and to America in partnership
with mentor-leaders like Dr. King,
seeking to serve God and a cause bigger than ourselves.*

—MARIAN WRIGHT EDELMAN

*December 21, 1956 — The Montgomery boycott
ends with the desegregation of city buses.*

discord

January 1957 — Black ministers form the Southern Christian Leadership Conference (SCLC). King is elected president and travels 780,000 miles and gives 208 speeches to help organize and support Civil Rights demonstrations around the country.

A lot of people thought that Dr. King was
an old man when he started,
but he was just 26 years old when he
led the Montgomery bus boycott,
and a lot of the Civil Rights movement
was led by young people.
Even in Birmingham, Alabama, when
young people were being sprayed by fire hoses
and bitten by police dogs, some of those children in those
marches ranged in age from 6 years old to 18 or 20.
So it can give people of my generation inspiration to say,
"OK, you don't have to wait 'til you're 30 or 40 years old.
You can begin the process now."

—JEREMY PONDS

discord

We entered seminary together, at Crozer in Chester, Pennsylvania.
There were only 11 of us black students at this white school. We had to make the
adjustment, and that was very difficult for those from the Deep South. He had not
been accustomed to sitting at the same table as whites, and this was an example of
what he hoped America would come to.
Everybody was under the spell of change, and when he entered seminary he said,
"We're going to change this nation."
God led him to Montgomery. I told him not to go. I'm eight years older, and I told him
he could get a better church in the North and he said, "That's where I'm needed. I'm
going South." Then when I saw that little church (Dexter), I saw that God had a hand
in it. God brought a Ph.D. to trouble the waters and it's been rippling ever since.

—THE REV. MARCUS GARVEY WOOD

I thought that he spoke about nonviolence,
but it seemed to me that violence seemed to follow in his footsteps.
And I suppose this is always the case in a situation like that.
I guess it was just my upbringing, but at the time I thought Martin Luther King, Jr.,
was an eloquent speaker, but a little too profound and in the limelight a lot.
And I guess it was a hangover from my redneck heritage,
but I felt like he was stirring things up. Looking back on it now,
I see that he was in the forefront, spearheading a movement
against something that probably should never have happened in the first place.
It's always easy to say that if he hadn't come down the pike
it would have happened some other way, and it probably would have.
But it would have taken more time, and it took courage on his part,
and on the part of others, too.

—DEAN STOKES

discord

I grew up in New Jersey, and I remember going to
Woolworth's and it was like the Promised Land.
My mother would go shopping and then we would buy a hamburger.
In the summer of 1958 or '59, I went to North Carolina to visit relatives.
We were walking along, and I went running ahead because I saw
Woolworth's and I'm thinking, "It's hamburger time!"
When I got in the door these big white hands picked me up
and pulled me to the colored section where you had to stand to eat.
And I remember a Woolworth's burger just never tasted the same again.
Interestingly enough, many years later, while at the Smithsonian,
I helped to bring the Woolworth lunch counter to the
American History Museum.

—LONNIE BUNCH

I remember when you couldn't go in the stores,
when you couldn't shop, when you couldn't drink at the water fountains.
They had water fountains saying
"White" and "Colored," and all of that.
I remember it very well.
The thing about Dr. King was he was a man of greatness and fortitude,
and you thought if he could do it, other people could, too.
And that would enhance me, make me a better woman and a better person,
and the world would be a better place.

—SHIRLEY MOREHEAD SIMMONS

discord

Dr. King and I and maybe two or three other men were standing in the lobby of a hotel in Birmingham. So here comes a well-groomed white man who had on a suit and a tie, nice shirt, looking like a successful businessman. He walked up to him and said, "Aren't you Martin Luther King?" And he said, "Yes, I am," and before Dr. King could ask him his name, he just drew back and—wham!—hit him upside the head and knocked him down.
I was really angry. I'm short in stature, and considered to be a little person, but I was so mad I wanted to grab him. And Dr. King said, "Now listen, you're forced to be nonviolent because you're too little to whip anybody." And we made a light-hearted moment of it, and Dr. King said, as he had before, that: "We've got to keep working and changing people's negative attitudes."

—XERNONA CLAYTON

I was one of the students who participated in the integration of the University of Tennessee in Knoxville. The restaurants and other public accommodations in and around the university that served the students were yet to be desegregated.
It was not always a pleasant experience, although it was not violent. You didn't have attack dogs and things like that, but mostly words, harsh language, name-calling, that kind of thing. And occasionally a grade marked down by a professor who wasn't willing to acknowledge that African-American students had the knowledge and the academic fortitude that other students had. Dr. King's emphasis on nonviolence and justice were important, because the students were ripe for recognizing that there were so many more possibilities if we were all accorded the same rights and responsibilities.

—MARION DELANEY-HARRIS

discord

We were products of the 1950s—everything was simple and uncomplicated.
There wasn't as much social consciousness then.
We had a maid named Cora Belle.
She worked seven days a week and made like $30.
She would wash and cook, and the clothes were hung out on the clothesline to dry.
She wore a white uniform and combed my hair, and we drank a lot of Coca-Colas.

She was at our house cooking at Thanksgiving and Christmas,
and I felt bad about that. It made me wonder what her family was doing,
and how she could take care of so many people.

If you're a regular person, and you're not tuned in to social change,
you just grew up in that environment. When Martin Luther King came along,
I didn't feel afraid. It was more like the world was going to change
and I didn't know how.

—MARY JANE STAFFORD THEDEN

June 23, 1958 — King, Roy Wilkins, A. Philip Randolph, and Lester Grange meet with President Dwight D. Eisenhower to discuss issues affecting black Americans.

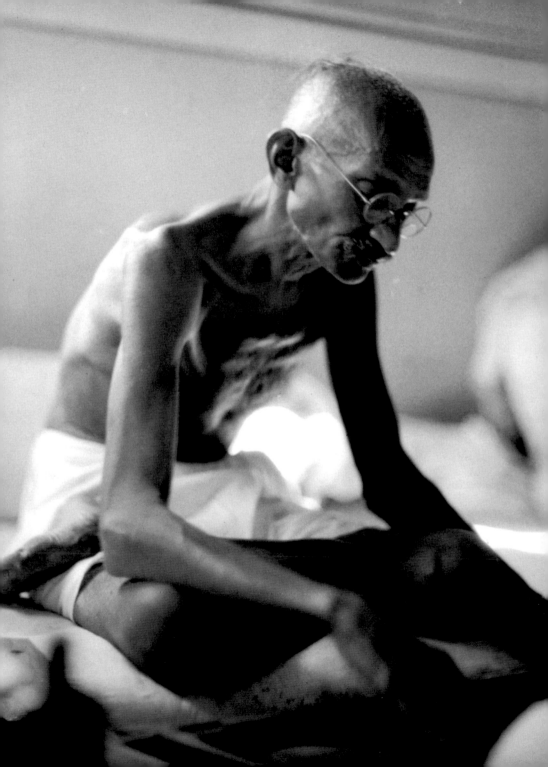

discord

In 1950, while at Crozer Theological Seminary,
King had gone into Philadelphia to hear a sermon on Gandhi
by Mordecai Johnson, president of Howard University,
and been so electrified that he bought and read
a half dozen books on Gandhi's life and works.
During that same period I had been reading
all of Gandhi's writings in English.
He had immersed himself in Gandhi and I was immersing myself.
I didn't know him and he didn't know me
but I started writing King
and was very active with him until he died.
He joked that I was the only lawyer in his midst who would tell
him to go to jail instead of using all my tricks to keep him out.

—HARRIS WOFFORD

In the midst of death, life persists. In the midst of darkness, light persists.

— KING'S FAVORITE QUOTE BY MAHATMA GANDHI

February 1959 — King goes to India where he meets Prime
Minister Jawaharlal Nehru and studies the passive
resistance techniques of Mohandas (Mahatma) Gandhi.
He also resigns from Dexter Avenue Baptist Church and
moves to Atlanta to concentrate on his SCLC activities.

The Storm is Passing Over

O courage, my soul, and let us journey on,
For tho' the night is dark, it won't be very long.
O thanks be to God, the morning light appears,
And the storm is passing over, Hallelujah!

O billows rolling high, and thunder shakes the ground,
The lightnings flash, and tempest all around,
But Jesus walks the sea and calms the angry waves,
And the storm is passing over, Hallelujah!

The stars have disappeared, and distant lights are dim,
My soul is filled with fears, the seas are breaking in.
I hear the Master cry, "Be not afraid, 'tis I,"
And the storm is passing over, Hallelujah!

Charles A. Tindley

crescendo

1960-1963

The real significance of the MARCH,
and the speech, was that it changed ATTITUDES.
Righteous indignation against
racial DISCRIMINATION *became*
widespread after the March.
It led to a time so full of PROMISE *and*
ACHIEVEMENT. *You could feel it.*

Dorothy Height,
Chair/President Emerita
of the National Council of
Negro Women

crescendo

AS THE CIVIL RIGHTS movement escalated, the King family became more and more a target of harassment. King was threatened, arrested, and terrorized by a bomb tossed onto the front porch of his own home. Reassured by his wife, Coretta, however, King continued the work of the movement, saying that if he worried about personal safety, he would accomplish nothing. The quality of a man's life, not longevity, he said, was most important.

In the late 1950s and early 1960s, King organized protests, and encouraged demonstrators to stand up for what he considered to be the best in the American Dream. He helped lay the groundwork for the SCLC, and in 1957 was not only listed in *Who's Who in America* but also made the cover of *Time* magazine. King completed his first book, *Stride Toward Freedom*, become co-pastor (with his father) of Atlanta's Ebenezer Baptist Church, and led a mass protest for fair hiring practices.

In 1963, King went to Birmingham to urge the desegregation of department stores there. The world was stunned by the brutality of policemen using dogs and fire hoses against Birmingham marchers, and King himself was arrested. Still, his voice was not silenced. From a jail cell in solitary confinement, heartened by encouraging words to Coretta from President John F. Kennedy, he wrote a lengthy statement on scraps of paper. In this *Letter from Birmingham Jail*, King clarified why he felt "compelled to carry the gospel of freedom beyond my own hometown."

He carried that gospel to millions on Aug. 28, 1963, during the March on Washington for Jobs and Freedom. He would later remember the day of the March as a great shout for freedom reverberating across America. It was a shout that reached President Kennedy, the halls of Congress, whites and blacks converging on the nation's capital, and millions of viewers and listeners around the world.

Positioned in front of the Lincoln Memorial, under a clear blue summer sky, King delivered the most enduring speech of his career, passionately proclaiming, "I have a dream!"

Ebenezer Baptist Church — Atlanta

February 1960 — King becomes co-pastor, with his father, of Ebenezer Baptist Church in Atlanta.

I had the unique opportunity to actually have been a student of Martin Luther King's, when he taught a single class at Morehouse College. But like so many others, I was his "student" in the larger sense— and learned from him the values of patience, perseverance, and purposefulness.

—JULIAN BOND

When Martin Luther King, Jr., and the movement arrived in my hometown of Birmingham, Alabama, in the early 1960s I was elated. The movement offered a way to speak out meaningfully and change the segregated and unjust world we lived in. Inspired by the courage of hundreds of other high school students just like me, I marched, sang and watched the "Whites Only" signs come down. We read Gandhi, Frantz Fanon, listened to Malcolm X, and learned to say that we wanted more, far more, and not just for ourselves, but for people suffering injustice around the globe.

—JENNIFER LAWSON

October 19, 1960 — King is arrested at an Atlanta lunch counter sit-in and jailed.

crescendo

The Freedom Riders came into the bus station across from the justice
building. You could hear the screaming, hear baggage flying out the door.
Two young women skirted the beatings that were going on.
They made their way to the sidewalk, and a satellite crowd pummeled
them. One was getting punched and the other was getting jostled.
I leapt up on the curb in my car and said, "Get in the back!"
I pulled one of them by the wrist and she said,
"Mister I don't want you to get hurt."
Then one of the crowd came up and I said the magic words:
"Get back. I'm with the federal government."
And he hit me in the head with a pipe.
A lieutenant took me to the hospital.
By Friday I was ready to get out so they took me to the airport
to catch a Delta, and it was the same plane that brought Martin in.
He came over to say, "I'm glad you're all right. I know it was a tough
time." That was a gesture he didn't have to make.

—JOHN SEIGENTHALER

October 16, 1962 — King meets President Kennedy
and urges his support of Civil Rights measures.

When I think about Dr King, I realize he was one of the first black faces
that I saw on television that was poised, smart, and ripe with leadership.
I was struck by how clearly he called for equality, and I marveled at the
bravery of all those who faced dogs, hoses, and racists filled with hate.
In many ways, King and those who struggled during the Civil Rights
movement helped me to believe that change was possible.

—LONNIE BUNCH

April 12, 1963 —
King is arrested during
a demonstration against
hiring practices and
segregated department
stores in Birmingham,
Alabama.

April 16, 1963 —
King writes his "Letter
from Birmingham Jail."

May 3–5, 1963 —
Police violence against
Birmingham protestors
focuses national attention
on segregation.

May 10, 1963 — Agreement
reached that desegregates stores,
schools, and restaurants,
and implements fair hiring
practices in Birmingham.

*I'm from Cleveland, Ohio, and my mother and I attended the
March on Washington, D.C., together. I was about 25 at the time.
When I heard him give the "I Have a Dream" speech, it was breathtaking.
I've never been in anything of that magnitude before.
The crowd was orderly, the people were attentive. As a child,
I never had a bed to sleep on. I slept on a plastic cot in the dining room.
We were very poor. But my grandmother kept telling me: "You can be anything you
want to be," and it was so true. I've come a long way from not having a bed to sleep
in—and that all has to go back to this man preaching equality, love, justice.*

—EUGENIA BREWER

August 28, 1963 — More than 200,000 participate in the March on Washington and hear King's "I Have a Dream" speech.

He may as well have been singing.
I was by the Reflecting Pool, and I knew at the time
I was hearing a historic speech. I looked at all of these
people and tears were running down their faces.
It was a stirring moment.
He realized, though, that he was not reaching that throng,
so he pushed the speech aside and preached.
He suddenly got in pitch, and by repeating that refrain,
he had his theme.
It is one of the great American speeches. It moved the country.

—GENE PATTERSON

crescendo

Of all the people there, Mahalia Jackson was the only superstar.
She was the one who knew crowds. King would come and do what he came to do
and do it very well, but it was Mahalia who sensed (near the end of King's speech)
that the crowd had not been satisfied. She called him Doc, and she said,
"Doc, Doc, tell them about the dream!"
It was a wonderful speech but she knew that it did not
come up to what the people needed.
What is amazing to me, though, is that through all of that—
some hundreds of thousands of people—he heard her.
And, of course, he had perfect cadence and he didn't miss a beat.
"And so I say to you..."—he just had to pull it up.
He was a preacher.
You open your mouth and the Lord will put the words in it.
He responded to the call of his flock.

—NIKKI GIOVANNI

crescendo

*Because of the March, because of the involvement of hundreds and
thousands of ordinary citizens, we experienced what I like to call
a nonviolent revolution under the rule of law—
a revolution of values, a revolution of ideas.
We have come a great distance toward laying down the burden of race and class,
but we still have a great distance to go.*

—CONGRESSMAN JOHN LEWIS

---

*I realize now that King made a courageous choice as he approached the end of his
prepared text. As a gifted orator intuitively able to respond to the mood of his
audience, he must have understood that his prepared remarks were intellectually
cogent but emotionally insufficient. ... Only after studying King's life could I begin
to understand his sudden decision to deliver the extemporaneous remarks that
would become imprinted on the nation's collective memory.
It was a brave choice but also one that was consistent with
his earlier experiences as a preacher and protest leader.*

—CLAYBORNE CARSON

---

*I think most people think of (Dr. King) as such a symbol and brilliant and all that.
The thing that I always think of is he was so down to earth
and he related to people so well. I remember one time the Civil Rights leadership
group had been meeting at a motel on a mountain so he would be away from the
press, and he had to go to Switzerland. Andy Young was driving.
As time got short, Andy Young was driving faster and faster, and he (Dr. King) said,
"Hold on there, Andy. I know they say they'll honor us more in death than in life
but don't try it now!" He had a sense of humor.
He was a real person. I think people need to know that.*

—DOROTHY HEIGHT

crescendo

WASHINGTON—The March was ended. The marble Lincoln
brooded over meadows snowy white with litter and placards.
In the sudden silence left by 200,000 departed people, the meaning of what
had happened here slowly settled into shape. It may have been historic.
It may be that this will be marked down as the date when the
Civil Rights movement grew up. ... But it still would have been just a
large turnout of people who came and heard predictable things
if Martin Luther King had not gotten carried away to spontaneity by
the roars of an electrified crowd. In a few impassioned and triumphant
moments below the great seated statue of Abraham Lincoln, King swept
the marchers to a new vision of the Negro's destiny in America by praising
and celebrating America, and lifting their eyes from the
"valley of despair" to purple mountain majesties.

"I have a dream," he boomed, again and again, and each dream showed
him liberty and pursuit of happiness for all races of Americans soon,
from the cliffs of the Rockies to the slopes of the Alleghenies,
from Stone Mountain in Georgia to the broad Mississippi.
"I have a dream," he roared, weeping, and his dream stretched
from sea to shining sea, and all the way from the speaker's
stand at the Lincoln Memorial to the far end of a crowd
that stretched to the Washington Monument.

—GENE PATTERSON, EDITOR, *ATLANTA CONSTITUTION*,
AUG. 30, 1963

September 15, 1963 — Bomb kills four young girls
and injures other worshippers at the Sixteenth Street
Baptist Church in Birmingham.

Lift Every Voice and Sing

Lift every voice and sing, till earth and Heaven ring,
Ring with the harmonies of liberty;
Let our rejoicing rise, high as the listening skies,
Let it resound loud as the rolling sea.
Sing a song full of the faith that the dark past has taught us,
Sing a song full of the hope that the present has brought us;
Facing the rising sun of our new day begun,
Let us march on till victory is won.

James Weldon Johnson

March toward

harmony

1964–1967

President Lyndon Johnson,
signing the Voting Rights Act.

*The central fact of American civilization—
one so hard for others to understand—is that
FREEDOM and JUSTICE and the DIGNITY of man
are not just words to us. We BELIEVE in them.
Under all the growth and the tumult and
abundance, we believe.*

1964, Nobel Ceremony

December 10, 1964 — King accepts the Nobel Peace Prize.

I still believe that we shall overcome.

—MARTIN LUTHER KING, JR.
NOBEL PEACE PRIZE SPEECH

Dr. King is probably the only one, or one of a few, who had no other reason to do what he did. He didn't do it for money. He did it because it was right. You know, he got the Nobel Prize money, and gave it all away, which was such a noble thing for him to do.

—XERNONA CLAYTON

TIME MAGAZINE NAMED KING its 1963 "Man of the Year." Soon afterward, with what he described as "emotions about to overflow," King also accepted the 1964 Nobel Peace Prize. The '60s, however, were to be years of political and social turmoil.

On June 12,1963, NAACP leader Medgar Evers was murdered, and less than a month after King's "I Have a Dream" speech, four young black girls were killed in a bombing at Birmingham's Sixteenth Street Baptist Church. Then, in November, President John F. Kennedy was assassinated, flooding the country with what King called a cascading grief. James Meredith, the first black student at the University of Mississippi, was wounded by a sniper in 1966, and two years later, a Memphis march was disrupted by violence.

Still, a time of great accomplishment was at hand. On July 2, 1964, President Lyndon Johnson signed the Civil Rights Act of 1964, and, a year later, the Voting Rights Act of 1965 became law.

King focused on the problems of the poor, reminding his children during morning devotions not to forget "the least of these." But he believed that what he characterized as a pessimistic clamor had been stilled by the "music of major victories."

I was very much inspired by Dr. King. At this time, it was the ending of the Jim Crow era where we had to go to the back of the bus, and I could see things opening up. We could eat at lunch counters, and people were beginning to vote. In the march from Selma to Montgomery, we had no trouble getting there.

But once we got there, the police had men on horses all around us, and they wouldn't allow us to leave, even to go to the bathroom.

But it changed my life.

It made me proud as a black person.

It showed me that I wasn't limited to the black society.

There was a whole world I could participate in.

—EARNEST BUSH

I never met Dr. King, but he was a powerful force in my life. I was in Tarboro, North Carolina, in 1957 when he came to his might. I loved the community but, racially, it was totally stratified. I served two of the three Episcopal churches in town—one populated by the owners of the mill in town and the professional whites and the other in the black section. Dr. King made it possible for me to grow, because when you take on the power structure of a tiny little Southern town that is thoroughly entrenched, you can be marginalized pretty quickly. I remember the Selma march in particular. I wish I'd gone there myself, but I probably didn't have enough courage.

—BISHOP JOHN SHELBY SPONG

March 7, 1965 — Marchers demanding voting rights for blacks are attacked outside Selma and chased into a housing project where residents are also beaten. The incident becomes known as "Bloody Sunday."

Martin lived at a time when it wasn't just the racists who were out to get you.
At the time, even under the Kennedys, the FBI wasn't always your best friend.
The eyes of J. Edgar Hoover were always on the movement.
But Martin never had any bodyguards around him.
He wasn't in a cocoon or an armed camp. He was a nonviolent man, and
basically believed that his moral authority, his soul force, was enough to guard him.
He didn't want security or bodyguards with guns to protect him.

—TOM HOUCK

March 21, 1965 —
King and 3,200 protesters
begin another march protected
by National Guardsmen. The
demonstration swells to 25,000
when marchers reach Montgomery.

In 1963 in Birmingham and in 1965 in Selma,
King sensed that nonviolent protest carried out
with sacrificial dedication could overcome what
others saw as insurmountable white opposition
at the local level and shaky support at the
Federal level. Between 1965 and 1968,
he endured consistent criticism for his crusades
against racism in Northern cities, economic injustice throughout the nation, and finally the tragic
war in Vietnam. To be a prophetic visionary and
to be courageous enough to pursue that vision in
the face of death is a rare thing in any realm of
human experience and perhaps even rarer in the
arena of politics and social justice. That is why
Martin Luther King, Jr., will be seen as the most
significant public figure to emerge from the Deep
South in the 20th Century and a fully credentialed
member of an American pantheon that starts
with the Founding Fathers.

—HOWELL RAINES

August 6, 1965 —
President Johnson signs
the Voting Rights Act,
prohibiting literacy
tests and poll taxes
and ensuring blacks
the right to vote.

1965

Voter Registration Line — Selma, 1965

*There are two things that showed his ability to cope
with tough realities in the midst of great danger.
First of all, he kept a tremendous sense of humor.
Secondly, he had a great desire to touch the people he saw
as on the lower end of the totem pole of our society.
When people wanted to stop and talk to him, he stopped and talked.
He was a hand shaker, and even after he was stabbed in Harlem,
that didn't cause him to pull back, because of his love of people.
That was a tremendous gift. That shows where he was in his heart and his
mind. He felt that he was in God's hands. He did it, and he did it with joy.*

— CAROLE F. HOOVER

51

harmony

My best memory of Martin came in the summer of 1966 when he was in Chicago at the time a riot broke out. President Johnson sent John Doar, head of the Civil Rights Division of Justice, and me to Chicago to do something about the riot.

When we got to the ragged building where he was living in Chicago, and as we trudged up the scarred and urine-smelling stairs, I thought of the cynics who thought Martin's promise to live in the ghetto was a play for the headlines. We got to the apartment and the room was choked with people squeezed into that little living room. I soon figured out that the people in the room were gang members— kids that the rest of the world feared and despised.

As I listened, I figured out that Martin was holding a teach-in on nonviolence with these tough kids who wanted to go out and take back their turf by throwing Molotov cocktails at the armored personnel carriers of the Illinois National Guard. If they had, a bunch of them would have been killed.

Martin was saving their lives and he stayed at it, answering every question that any of the kids felt like raising until he had taught the violence right out of them. And Martin wouldn't let them go until each of them promised to come by the next afternoon to get involved in some of the SCLC-sponsored activities. That was Martin doing his work quietly with no outside witnesses—Martin in the raw, you might say; just teaching nonviolence and bettering the lives of poor black kids.

—ROGER WILKINS

January 22, 1966 — King moves into a Chicago tenement to bring attention to living conditions of the poor.

harmony

Sometimes conscience dictates that you take a position that is neither safe,
nor politic, nor popular, but you must take it because it is right.
This is where I find myself today.
I have come to the conclusion that the ultimate measure of a man is not where
he finds himself in moments of comfort and moments of convenience,
but where he finds himself in moments of challenge and moments of controversy.
It is my great hope that the dark clouds of war will soon pass away
and the deep fog of misunderstanding will be lifted from our fear-drenched world,
and in some not too distant tomorrow the radiant stars of peace and
brotherhood will shine over our great nation and the world.

—MARTIN LUTHER KING, JR.
LETTER TO GENE PATTERSON, MAY 10, 1967

November 27, 1967 — King, who said he refused to play
it safe, announces the Poor People's Campaign and another
march on Washington. His goal: a $12-billion Economic
Bill of Rights that would guarantee everyone employment
and income, and end housing discrimination.

In the spring of 1968 I was the federal official assigned to work with SCLC to pave the
way for the Poor People's Campaign to come to Washington. I'd had talks with Martin
and some of his aides and after the first blow-up in Memphis I called him about set-
ting up another meeting, and he said he had to go back to Memphis. I told him I
thought that was a bad idea and asked him why he thought he needed to go. He said:
"I promised them." So he went back to Memphis to keep his promise to some of
the most despised workers in America, the sanitation men of Memphis.
Message: You never stop until the least is healed, or until you can't do it anymore.

—ROGER WILKINS

harmony

It may get me crucified.
I may even die.
But I want it said even if I die in the struggle that
"He died to make men free."

—MARTIN LUTHER KING, JR.

<hr/>

I interacted with King a couple of times in the Nashville sit-in movement, but it was brief. The first time I got a chance to see him up close
was with Bob Kennedy in April. Bob made an appeal for King to focus
on voter registration. He said, "If I can get these cases into court, I can
win them." Bob was the ultimate pragmatist, but King was the ultimate
idealist. He said he really must confront racism wherever it exists,
that he must do it in a way that dramatizes the evil.
He said to me, "You will remember the sit-ins in Nashville. The change
would not have come there if your paper, The Tennessean, had not been
willing to focus on the students sitting at the lunch counters."
It was not a lecture.
It was a passionate statement about what drove him.

—JOHN SEIGENTHALER

Amazing Grace

Amazing Grace! How sweet the sound
That saved a wretch like me!
I once was lost, but now am found
Was blind, but now I see.

'Twas Grace that taught my heart to fear,
And Grace my fears relieved.
How precious did that Grace appear
The hour I first believed.

Through many dangers, toils, and snares
I have already come.
'Tis Grace hath brought me safe thus far
And Grace will lead me home.

John Newton

elegy

1968-1969

Death comes to every individual.

There is an amazing DEMOCRACY *about death. It*

is not ARISTOCRACY *for some of the people, but a*

democracy for all of the people.

...Death is the irreducible COMMON

DENOMINATOR *of all men.*

Martin Luther King, Jr.,
eulogy for victims of Sixteenth
Street Baptist Church bombing

1968 Sanitation Strike

March 1968 — Memphis Sanitation Workers' Strike

Dr. King believed that America could provide a roof over every citizen's head, an education for their minds, a job to support their families, and freedom to pray and grow and sing and worship and feed their spirit. He led us towards that land promised in the Declaration of Independence but could not stay to go with us. But in Memphis in his last speech he promised us we would get there. It is time for us to cross over.

—MARIAN WRIGHT EDELMAN

elegy

ON APRIL 3, 1968, Martin Luther King, Jr., delivered his last address, the historic "Been to the Mountaintop" speech at the Bishop J. Mason Temple in Memphis. King spoke of hearing the voice of freedom crying through time: "It may not come today or it may not come tomorrow, but it is well that it is within thine heart. It's well that you are trying."

He challenged listeners to dream of a better day, and to recognize God working in the 20th century.

King, who had encouraged Memphis sanitation workers to sweep the city streets as Michelangelo painted pictures, Beethoven composed music, and Shakespeare wrote poetry, also told them to stand determined in their strike. Recalling the time when he had been knifed in New York during a book-signing, King, who believed he had "divine companionship" in his life, assured listeners that he was not afraid to die.

The next day, April 4, 1968, at about 6 p.m., King was shot and killed as he stood on the balcony of the Lorraine Motel. Five days later, some 100,000 people gathered in Atlanta to attend King's funeral services or pay their respects along the lengthy funeral procession. The casket, carried in a wooden farm wagon drawn by two mules, was taken to South-View Cemetery, a 19th-century, historically black cemetery.

"If physical death was the price he had to pay to rid America of prejudice and injustice, nothing could be more redemptive," said Benjamin E. Mays in a eulogy. "Martin Luther King's unfinished work on Earth must truly be our own."

Some bystanders watched in silence. A few sang freedom songs. Others cried.

Recalled friend and colleague Harris Wofford: "At a mass meeting, he had said, 'If one day you find me sprawled out dead, I do not want you to retaliate with a single act of violence.'"

March 29, 1968 — King leads 6,000 marchers in support of a sanitation workers' strike in Memphis. But violence between bystanders and police, the death of a demonstrator, and rioting force the occupation of the city by 4,000 National Guardsmen.

elegy

Martin Luther King dedicated his life to love and to justice between fellow human beings. He died because of that effort. In this difficult day, in this difficult time for the United States, it's perhaps well to ask what kind of a nation we are and what direction we want to move in. For those of you who are black— considering the evidence evidently is that there were white people who were responsible—you can be filled with bitterness, and with hatred, and a desire for revenge.

We can move in that direction as a country, in greater polarization—black people amongst black, and the white amongst white, filled with hatred toward one another. Or we can make an effort, as Martin Luther King did, to understand and to comprehend, and replace that violence, that stain of bloodshed that has spread across our land, with an effort to understand compassion and love. ... What we need in the United States is not division; what we need in the United States is not hatred; what we need in the United States is not violence or lawless- ness, but is love and wisdom, compassion toward one another, and a feeling of justice toward those who still suffer within our country, whether they be white or whether they be black.

—ROBERT F. KENNEDY

I've heard some people say: "Martin was never afraid." That's nuts. From the time around 1955 when somebody tried to blow up his house until the day he died, Martin knew that there were people out there who wanted to kill him. Every morning when he woke up over those 13 years, he knew they were out there. Not to feel fear in that situation, he would have had to have been crazy.

Martin wasn't crazy, and he got up in the morning and went out and did what he had to do. To know that mortal danger is lurking and to do your work anyway—that's seriously brave.

—ROGER WILKINS

elegy

I never met Dr. King but was always impressed
by his passion and dedication to unity.
The last sermon he preached in 1968 before going
to Memphis was at the National Cathedral.
I was literally across the driveway at St. Alban's,
and we had hooked up a P.A. system
from the Cathedral. We stopped our service
and turned on the speakers to hear Dr. King.
He was a powerful presence.

—NORMAN SCRIBNER

April 3, 1968 — Speaking at the Bishop J. Mason
Temple in Memphis, King gives his famous
"I've Been to the Mountaintop" speech.

April 4, 1968 — While standing on the balcony of the Lorraine Motel in Memphis, King is shot and killed.

elegy

I was a grad student at the University of Pennsylvania.
We were at a dinner and someone called me over and she said,
"King has been shot," and I knew he hadn't been shot, he had been killed.
And I said, "I'm going." I picked up a couple of friends and we decided
to drive. When we got in line to view the body at Ebenezer (church),
we were right behind a busload of women who had come from Detroit.
They had been traveling since God knows when.
A security person said, "Aren't you Nikki Giovanni?" and then he said,
"You can come with me and come into the church."
I said I was with these women from Detroit and said I wouldn't do it.
I didn't think the people who marched with King should be excluded.
I rejected it because the whole point of Martin Luther King
was the women I was standing with—those women who loved King.

—NIKKI GIOVANNI

1968 — Violence erupts in more than 100 U.S. cities and some 20,000 are arrested. James Earl Ray is convicted of the assassination in March 1969, but later recants his confession.

elegy

On April 4, 1968, at the Atlanta airport, Coretta King
got the call that she says she had subconsciously been waiting
for all her life. Her husband "had felt a mystical identity
with the spirit and meaning of Christ's Passion," and
she felt it somewhat strange, yet somehow
appropriate, that his death should come in the week before
Easter. Before going to Memphis, in his last sermon at the
Ebenezer Baptist Church, Martin King had spoken of his
own death, saying, "I don't want a long funeral"; he asked
for it to be said only that "Martin Luther King, Jr., tried to
give his life serving others ... tried to love somebody ...
tried to be right on the war question."

The funeral with its many eulogies was far from short,
but he would have approved the long march. ...
"We marched at his funeral," Coretta King explained,
"because Martin had spent so much of his life marching ...
This was his last great march."

—HARRIS WOFFORD

The Funeral of Martin Luther King, Jr.
His headstone said
FREE AT LAST, FREE AT LAST
But death is a slave's freedom
We seek the freedom of free men
And the construction of a world
Where Martin Luther King could have lived
And preached nonviolence

—NIKKI GIOVANNI

elegy

Television doesn't quite close the distance.
You've got to be inside the Ebenezer Baptist Church,
among this intensely human family called the Negro people,
as they sing, "Softly and tenderly, Jesus is calling"
over the body of their dead brother—among them in the heat
of the little church where tears mingle with perspiration
and the lips of the choir singers tremble.

You've got to sit between the mourners and touch shoulders
with them in the crowd and feel the heat come up through
your shoes from the hot pavement as you march with them
behind the casket drawn, with perfect fitness,
by a two-mule wagon. ...

You have to be there in the pews for
the funeral of Martin Luther King, Jr.
to know the full truth—that we whites have committed
the monstrous wrong of thrusting away a people
we do not even know, and hurting them out of our
fear born of our ignorance. ...

Knowing and loving our neighbors is
the needed memorial to Dr. King.
And that is so easy, when you are among them.

—GENE PATTERSON, EDITOR,
ATLANTA CONSTITUTION, APRIL 10, 1968

Let All the World in Every Corner Sing

Let all the world in every corner sing, my God and King!
The heavens are not too high, His praise may thither fly,
the Earth is not too low, His praises there may grow.
Let all the world in every corner sing, my God and King!

Let all the world in every corner sing, my God and King!
The church with psalms must shout,
no door can keep them out;
but, above all, the heart must bear the longest part.
Let all the world in every corner sing, my God and King!

George Herbert and Martin F. Shaw

symphony

of brotherhood

*This is our hope. This is the faith with which
I return to the South ... With this faith we will
be able to transform the jangling* DISCORD
of our nation into a beautiful SYMPHONY
of brotherhood.

Martin Luther King, Jr.

73

Symphony

One of Dr. King's great legacies was his vision of a "symphony of brotherhood." Born into a long line of distinguished Southern preachers, he knew the power of words and music and used them to inspire the men, women, and children who suffered for Civil Rights.

Almost a half a century after his death, King's voice can still be heard—resounding through books, videos, audiotapes, and dramas, as well as in the centers and exhibits that continue his work.

The King Center was dedicated in 1982. Congress designated the third Monday in January as Martin Luther King Day. And for some 20 years, The Choral Arts Society of Washington has offered a special concert honoring him in the John F. Kennedy Center for the Performing Arts, the nation's premier cultural center.

In addition, a memorial to King is scheduled to take its place soon on the National Mall in Washington, D.C., where King once proclaimed, "I have a dream!"

Most of all, however, King's message is being passed down through the generations—from adults who recall King's courage and leadership, to youngsters just discovering his teachings.

"He showed me that one man can make a difference if he puts his mind to something," said Cameron Crumley, a Georgia middle-school student, after viewing an Atlanta History Center exhibit of King's papers. "If you want to do something badly enough, you can do it."

Still, for King's work to continue, it must be preserved by everyone who honors his ideals.

"We cannot wait or hope for another Martin," noted King's fraternity brother, Darryl R. Matthews, Sr. "We must become Martin."

April 1968 — Less than a week after King's death, Congress passes the Fair Housing Act he had campaigned for. It prohibits discrimination in the sale or rental of housing on the basis of race, color, religion, or national origin.

I Still Believe

I still believe that people should not struggle in violence.
Instead we should show peace in silence.

I still believe that Dr. King was right:
We should not settle disagreements with a fight.

I still believe that we should march in peace.
We should be able to visit any restaurant that we choose, to feast.

I still believe that we should love our enemies.
We should be free to be a doctor, a teacher, or sail the Seven Seas.

I still believe that little black kids should receive an education
So that we can learn geography, science, and multiplication.

I still believe that we should not fight with our fists
But instead we should settle our arguments with a kiss.

I still believe, I still believe
That we should all band together—blacks and whites—to achieve.

David Garris, 9 years old

*Dr. King spoke to something deeply human, which transcended
race, ethnicity, nationality, and politics. At the same time he was
able to speak to and communicate with those of little formal
education as well as those holding multiple university degrees.
As a moral, spiritual leader, Dr. Martin Luther King, Jr.,
was a leader of the people. All the people!*

—BISHOP WOODIE W. WHITE

Symphony

What he did, what he said, and what he sacrificed inspired an entire genera-tion, and its power still rings throughout this nation and the world. We are a different country today. We are a better people today; we are a better people today because Martin Luther King, Jr., believed in the power of love over hate, the power of nonviolence over violence, and the power of peace over war.

—CONGRESSMAN JOHN LEWIS

He taught by example that true change must come with each of us, and begins with each of us and that, love, not violence, is the most powerful force for social change. Dr. King was surrounded by bigotry and hate, and, yet, he never stopped believing in the enduring power of love.

—FIRST LADY LAURA BUSH

Little did he know that his life would change our lives. His was a life that changed a nation. I was, and shall ever remain, moved by his passion, his purpose, and his power ... for through his words we are admonished to think of others—before we think of ourselves.

—DARRYL R. MATTHEWS, SR.

Most Americans remember Dr. King as a great leader. I do, too. But I also remember him as someone able to admit how often he was afraid and unsure of his next step. But faith prevailed over fear and uncertainty and fatigue and depression. It was his human vulnerability and his ability to rise above it that I most remember. In this, he was not different from many Black adults whose credo has been to make "a way out of no way."

—MARIAN WRIGHT EDELMAN

Martin Luther King's words and actions still resonate because they are not simply a piece of history: They apply directly and powerfully to the problems we face today. His speech against the war in Vietnam could easily refer to the war in Iraq. He understood that political and Civil Rights would not be enough to guarantee equality—that a fundamental change in our economic system was necessary for a just society.

—HOWARD ZINN

Symphony

Even as I remind students about the freedom struggles that King inspired, I am pleased that a new generation of African Americans no longer bears the pain of Jim Crow segregation and young Asians and Africans no longer remember life under colonialism and apartheid.

—CLAYBORNE CARSON

I still believe in Dr. Martin Luther King, Jr.,'s work. His hard work lets people have a chance for a peaceful future. He wanted other people to believe in nonviolence. He wanted people to work together. He did not want people to kill each other.
Dr. King's hard work will help us get a good education. I will have a better career in the future because I can go to good schools. It may help me be a lawyer and help change laws to help people, too. It may help me to be a hero.

—DAQUAYE WELLS

October 10, 1980 — The 23-acre Martin Luther King, Jr., Historic Site is designated a National Historic Site.

January 15, 1982 — The building housing the Martin Luther King, Jr., Center for Non-Violent Change, known as the King Center, is dedicated on King's birthday at the National Historic Site.

November 1986 — Congress designates the third Monday
in January as a day to honor Martin Luther King, Jr.

Symphony

The Nobel Prize also profoundly magnified the inspiring global influence of
Martin Luther King, Jr., the greatest leader that my native state has ever
produced. On a personal note, it is unlikely that my political career beyond
Georgia would have been possible without the changes brought about by the
Civil Rights movement in the American South and throughout our nation.
On the steps of our memorial to Abraham Lincoln, Dr. King said:
"I have a dream that on the red hills of Georgia the sons of former slaves
and the sons of former slave-owners will be able to sit down together at a
table of brotherhood." The scourge of racism has not been vanquished,
either in the red hills of our state or around the world. And yet we see ever
more frequent manifestations of his dream of racial healing.

—PRESIDENT JIMMY CARTER,
ACCEPTING THE 2002 NOBEL PEACE PRIZE

He made it possible for us to be able to vote, to go to museums and libraries.
So many more doors and job opportunities were opened to us, and better
housing and schools, too. I'm currently a member of the church that
his father and grandfather pastored, as well as Dr. King.
His presence is very much alive there.

—HATTIE HARRIS SHIPP

The life of Dr. King has provided the best tool of learning for me
imaginable. Returning over and over again to the complexity that was
his life, for the layers of connections his actions brought together, I am
constantly amazed at what I learn. Only now in my adulthood do I truly
appreciate a fuller meaning of the man who was able to convey the universal
experiences in the Civil Rights struggle to a world audience...and was,
in turn, recognized, supported and honored for that effort.

—ANGELA KEISER

Once I was meeting with Mary McLeod Bethune. A group of us young women were there and one of them turned and said, "Who is going to take our place when we're gone?" And we said, "Nobody. It is going to have to be everybody." I think this is something we have to spread. Dr. King's philosophy of nonviolence is even more relevant today.

—DOROTHY HEIGHT

Symphony

What King would want us to do is to start within our family, with the intelligence and education of our children. To inform them of what history has taught us and to educate them about great leaders —Gandhi, Kennedy, Lincoln, and Martin Luther King—and to take the lessons we learned, and instill them in their minds. The common denominator is love.

—TERRANCE JONES

We want to freeze Dr. King as that man at the Lincoln Memorial talking about a dream when he had a lot more depth to him than just that. Dr. King spoke about a variety of situations that we really see coming to pass now.
He said that the three evils of society are racism, poverty, and violence, and we see all three of those evils still working and inter-related. He said as long as those three evils exist, we still need organizations like the SCLC and people of all walks of life to come together and try to eradicate them. That's my mission.

— JEREMY PONDS

His inimitable oratory and courage continue to inspire us.

—ARCHBISHOP DESMOND TUTU

Symphony

I prepare meals for the homeless and work with the juvenile court system, helping families that are splitting up—children coming out of the home, mothers and fathers who need parenting skills, and what have you. I've always given back because of his philosophy.

— EUGENIA BREWER

King was always concerned about those who were excluded from the table of brotherhood and sisterhood. It did not matter if they were young, old or on the margins of society. His passion was to bring all people together in a symphony of love. He referred to this coming together of all of God's children as reconciliation. Reconciliation was the main key in which his advocacy for excluded persons was set. He understood the love of God as the power of reconciliation that unites races and fractured communities.

—NOEL LEO ERSKINE

The dream of Martin Luther King (was) to elevate the dignity of each person, the worth of each person, the freedom of each person to realize his or her dreams.

—PRESIDENT GEORGE W. BUSH

December 1999 — A site in Washington, D.C., is approved for a national memorial in King's honor.

Symphony

In the struggle for freedom, equality and justice, nonviolence, his passion for peace, is the most effective strategy. When the real battlefield is the human heart, civil disobedience works better than suicide bombing.

—PRESIDENT BILL CLINTON

Where do we go from here?

—MARTIN LUTHER KING, JR.

Epilogue

Once in a long while, an individual appears whose destiny is to be a beacon for the hopes and aspirations of many. Such a man was Martin Luther King, Jr.— devoted minister of God, charismatic advocate for universal civil rights, and tireless champion for the brotherhood and sisterhood of all peoples everywhere.

Dr. King will long be remembered for his extraordinary leadership on behalf of freedom and justice for black Americans. Following the teachings of Mahatma Gandhi, he appealed to blacks and whites alike to seek these goals through nonviolent means, an approach which yielded historic results. *Voices* chronicles Dr. King's remarkable journey in an eloquent and moving way, with memorable photographs, words, and song.

As the momentous years of the Civil Rights movement progressed, Dr. King's message reached out to embrace the entire world. His work lives on as an inspiring example to all races and creeds of how much can be accomplished through peaceful actions. As our world becomes more and more one interconnected family, his enduring words continue to resonate as the defining global imperative of our time.

The legacy of Martin Luther King, Jr., now belongs to the ages. Our children, and their children for generations to follow, will remember this gentle, strong, brilliant, and compassionate man who led us toward understanding and reconciliation among "all God's children." May we be ever mindful of his noble life as we renew our own commitment to his shining dream of peace and love for us all.

—NORMAN SCRIBNER
ARTISTIC DIRECTOR
THE CHORAL ARTS SOCIETY OF WASHINGTON

JULIAN BOND, a Civil Rights activist and former Georgia legislator, serves on the board of the Southern Poverty Law Center.

EUGENIA BREWER of Villa Rica, Georgia, is a retired finance manager who volunteers with juveniles and the homeless.

LONNIE BUNCH is Director of the National Museum of African American History and Culture.

EARNEST BUSH, a retired IRS employee from Decatur, Georgia, is Pastor of New Hope Baptist Church in Rydal, Georgia.

PRESIDENT GEORGE W. BUSH is the 43rd President of the United States.

LAURA BUSH, wife of President George W. Bush, is the First Lady of the United States.

CLAYBORNE CARSON is a Professor of History at Stanford University and Founding Director of the Martin Luther King, Jr., Research and Education Institute.

PRESIDENT JIMMY CARTER was the 39th President of the United States and winner of the 2002 Nobel Peace Prize.

XERNONA CLAYTON, a colleague and friend of the King family, is the creator and Executive Producer of the Trumpet Awards, which honor African-Americans and their achievements.

PRESIDENT BILL CLINTON was the 42nd President of the United States.

CAMERON CRUMLEY is a 14-year-old student at Crabapple Middle School in Roswell, Georgia.

MARION DELANEY-HARRIS of Atlanta is a retired management consultant, trainer, and college instructor.

MARIAN WRIGHT EDELMAN is an author, as well as founder and President of the Children's Defense Fund.

NOEL LEO ERSKINE is Associate Professor of Ethics and Theology at the Candler School of Theology at Emory University.

MAHATMA GANDHI was a Hindu nationalist leader and social reformer in India. Known for his belief in nonviolent civil disobedience and his leadership in helping India gain independence, Gandhi was assassinated in 1948.

DAVID GARRIS attends Kipp Academy in Washington, D.C.

NIKKI GIOVANNI is a poet, author, commentator, activist, and University Distinguished Professor at Virginia Tech.

DOROTHY HEIGHT is an educator, activist, and Chair/President Emerita of the National Council of Negro Women.

CAROLE F. HOOVER is President and CEO of Hoover Milstein in Cleveland and New York City.

TOM HOUCK, a former Civil Rights activist, is a principal in the Atlanta public affairs firm of Miller Houck.

PRESIDENT LYNDON JOHNSON was the 36th President of the United States.

TERRANCE JONES is a Public Health Scientist with the Centers for Disease Control and Prevention in Atlanta.

ANGELA KEISER is Coordinator of Special Projects at the Gilder Lehrman Center for the Study of Slavery, Resistance, & Abolition at The Whitney and Betty MacMillan Center for International and Area Studies at Yale. She is also Regional Coordinator of the UNESCO Transatlantic Slave Education Project.

ROBERT F. KENNEDY was the U.S. Attorney General from 1961-1964. He was also a U.S. Senator and brother of President John F. Kennedy.

JENNIFER LAWSON is General Manager of WHUT-TV, Howard University Television, in Washington, D.C., and a producer of documentaries.

U.S. REP. JOHN LEWIS, the youngest speaker at the1963 March on Washington, represents Georgia's 5th Congressional District.

DARRYL R. MATTHEWS, SR., is an official with the Martin Luther King, Jr., National Memorial project.

ROSA PARKS, was a seamstress in Montgomery, Alabama, who refused to give up her bus seat to a white passenger on Dec. 1, 1955. This act of defiance, and her arrest, is believed by many to have ignited the Civil Rights movement.

EUGENE PATTERSON, a retired journalist and professor, won the 1967 Pulitzer Prize for editorial writing while editor of the *Atlanta Constitution*.

JEREMY PONDS of Panama City, Florida, attended Morehouse College in Atlanta.

HOWELL RAINES is a Pulitzer Prize-winning journalist and former executive editor of *The New York Times*, as well as the author of several books.

NORMAN SCRIBNER is Artistic Director of The Choral Arts Society of Washington.

JOHN SEIGENTHALER, an award-winning journalist for *The Tennessean* and founding editorial director of *USA TODAY*, served in the U.S. Justice Department as Administrative Assistant to Attorney General Robert F. Kennedy. Seigenthaler also founded the First Amendment Center at Vanderbilt University.

HATTIE HARRIS SHIPP of College Park, Georgia, is a retired school official and deaconess at Ebenezer Baptist Church.

SHIRLEY MOREHEAD SIMMONS of Greensboro, North Carolina, is a retired chauffeur who teaches at black history seminars.

BISHOP JOHN SHELBY SPONG is the retired Episcopal bishop of Newark, New Jersey, and author of more than a dozen books.

DEAN STOKES develops and manages real estate in Atlanta.

MARY JANE STAFFORD THEDEN teaches piano and is on the board of directors of the Stafford Development Company in Georgia.

MAMIE TILL-MOBLEY, a teacher, the mother of Civil Rights victim Emmett Till and co-author of the book *Death of Innocence: The Story of the Hate Crime That Changed America*.

ARCHBISHOP DESMOND TUTU became the first black Archbishop of Cape Town in 1986, an office he held until his retirement in 1996. He won the 1984 Nobel Peace Prize.

DAQUAYE WELLS attends Lucy D. Slowe Elementary School in Washington, D.C.

BISHOP WOODIE W. WHITE is Bishop in Residence at the Candler School of Theology at Emory University.

ROGER WILKINS a former journalist and U.S. Assistant Attorney General, is a professor at George Mason University.

HARRIS WOFFORD served as Special Assistant on Civil Rights to President John F. Kennedy, Associate Director of the Peace Corps for President Lyndon Johnson, and a U.S. Senator. He teaches at the University of Maryland.

REV. MARCUS GARVEY WOOD, a seminary classmate of King's, is Co-Pastor of Providence Baptist Church in Baltimore.

HOWARD ZINN is a historian, playwright, activist, and Boston University Professor Emeritus.

ACKNOWLEDGMENTS

VOICES: Reflections on an American Icon Through Words and Song has been an extraordinary experience for everyone involved, and it could not have been accomplished without the help of many, many people.

First and foremost the publisher would like to personally thank Norman Scribner for embracing this project and sharing with us his tribute concert to Dr. King. The team of professionals we have worked with at The Choral Arts Society of Washington, especially Debra Kraft, Annie Keiser, Joe Holt, Jeff Hart, Stephanie Cronenberg, and Elizabeth Romig, have made this project a dream come true for all of us.

Thank you to all the children and adults from many different walks of life who graciously agreed to be interviewed for, or quoted in, this special book. Their remembrances of Dr. King, and reflections on his life, leadership, and courage in the face of adversity, are greatly appreciated, and their "voices" are now part of Civil Rights history.

Special thanks to Yvette Reyes at AP images for her assistance with photos for the book and to John Christensen and Neil Skene for their assistance with research and review of the text.

I am enormously grateful to all the staff at Dalmatian Press — our design, editorial, production, and sales teams—for their enthusiasm and commitment to this project. It was their collective efforts and putting in the time to go the extra mile that helped make this a truly extraordinary package.

Finally, may the words and music presented here further Dr. King's message to respect and embrace our cultural differences, so that we may live in a world of peace and harmony.

WORKS CITED

Call & Post newspaper, Mamie Till-Mobley quote, Sept. 18, 1955.

Carson, Clayborne, ed. *The Autobiography of Martin Luther King, Jr.* (Warner Books, Inc., 1998).

Carter, Jimmy. Nobel Peace Prize speech, 2002.

Clark, Roy Peter, and Arsenault, Raymond, eds. *The Changing South of Gene Patterson* (University Press of Florida, 2002).

Dorsey, Thomas A. *Precious Lord, Take My Hand.* ©1938 (Renewed) Warner-Tamerlane Publishing Corp. Used by permission of Alfred Publishing Co., Inc.

Edelman, Marian Wright. *Lanterns* (HarperCollins Publishers, Inc., 2000).

Edelman, Marian Wright. *The Measure of Our Success* (Beacon Press, 1992).

Garris, David. "I Still Believe."

Giovanni, Nikki. "The Funeral of Martin Luther King, Jr." *The Selected Poems of Nikki Giovanni* (William Morrow and Company, Inc., 1996).

Height, Dorothy. *Open Wide the Freedom Gates* (PublicAffairs, 2003).

Herbert, George and Shaw, Martin F. *Let All the World in Every Corner Sing.*

Hollinshead, Byron, ed. *I Wish I'd Been There* (Doubleday, 2006).

Johnson, James Weldon. *Lift Every Voice and Sing.*

Robert F. Kennedy. Remarks on the assassination of Martin Luther King, Jr.

King, Martin Luther, Jr. Letter to Eugene Patterson, May 10, 1967.

Lawson, Jennifer. *Veterans of the Civil Rights Movement* Web site.

Matthews, Darryl, Sr. Speech at groundbreaking of the Martin Luther King, Jr., National Memorial, Nov. 13, 2006.

Newton, John. *Amazing Grace.*

Eugene Patterson, editorials. ©2006 *The Atlanta Journal-Constitution.* Reprinted with permission from *The Atlanta Journal-Constitution.*

Tindley, Charles A. *The Storm is Passing Over.*

We Shall Overcome. (Traditional).

Wofford, Harris. *Of Kennedys & Kings, Making Sense of the Sixties* (University of Pittsburgh Press, 1980).

Wood, Rev. Marcus Garvey. *And Grace Will Lead Me Home* (Gateway Press, Inc., 1998).

Voices

A Choral Tribute to
Dr. Martin Luther King, Jr.

A Compilation of Performances (1989-2007) Recorded Live at
The John F. Kennedy Center for the Performing Arts – Washington, DC

1. *Lift Every Voice and Sing* 4:34 (1997)
(J. Rosamond Johnson)
Rev. Nolan Williams, Jr., conductor
The Choral Arts Society of Washington –
  Norman Scribner, Artistic Director
The Eleanor Roosevelt High School Chamber and
  Women's Choirs – Dr. Barbara Baker, Music Director
The Young Adult Fellowship Ensemble of Metropolitan
  Baptist Church – Rev. Nolan Williams, Jr. and
  Richard Smallwood, Co-Music Directors
Ralph Alan Herndon, piano; William Neil, pipe organ;
Washington Symphonic Brass

2. *Let All the World in Every Corner Sing* 3:55 (1993)
(Ralph Vaughan Williams)
Norman Scribner, conductor
The Choral Arts Society of Washington –
  Norman Scribner, Artistic Director
Fred Begun, timpani; David Flowers, trumpet;
William Huckaby, pipe organ; Keith Jones, trumpet

3. *Born to Die* 7:03 (1989)
(Glenn Edward Burleigh)
Edward Jackson, conductor
The Duke Ellington School of the Arts Concert Choir and
  The DC Youth Chorale and Alumni –
  Edward Jackson, Music Director
Arphelius Paul Gatling, Gwendalyn Jackson and
Anthony Leach, keyboards

4. *Guide My Feet* 6:08 (2005)
(Avis D. Graves)
Arphelius Paul Gatling, conductor
Josepha Hammond, soprano; LaMar Hortman, baritone
The Martin Luther King Tribute Choir* –
  Arphelius Paul Gatling, Music Director
Earnest Hargrove, pipe organ; Ralph Alan Herndon, piano;
Jimmy Russell, drums; Christopher Suggs, electric bass

5. *I Know I've Been Changed* 3:27 (2002)
(arr. Damon Dandridge)
Dr. Barbara Baker, conductor
Ruby M. Robertson, soprano
The Choral Arts Society of Washington –
  Norman Scribner, Artistic Director

6. *The Storm is Passing Over* 3:00 (1996)
(arr. Donald Vails and Dr. Barbara Baker)
Joan Gregoryk, conductor
The Chevy Chase Elementary School Chorus –
  Joan Gregoryk, Music Director
Everett P. Williams, Jr., piano

7. *Deep River* 2:59 (1991)
(arr. Harry T. Burleigh)
Norman Scribner, conductor
The Choral Arts Society of Washington –
  Norman Scribner, Artistic Director

8. *Goin' Up to Glory* 2:20 (1997)
(Andre J. Thomas)
Dr. Barbara Baker, conductor
The Eleanor Roosevelt High School Chamber and
  Women's Choirs – Dr. Barbara Baker, Music Director
Deni Foster, piano

9. *The Downward Road is Crowded* 2:57 (2006)
(arr. Phillip McIntyre)
Linda Edge Gatling, conductor
Stephanie Sylver, mezzo-soprano
The Martin Luther King Tribute Choir* –
  Linda Edge Gatling, Music Director

10. *Blessed Assurance* 5:15 (2007)
(Traditional)
Anita C. Smith, conductor
The Choral Arts Society of Washington –
  Norman Scribner, Artistic Director
The Martin Luther King Tribute Choir* –
  Linda Edge Gatling, Music Director
The Duke Ellington School of the Arts Show Choir –
  Samuel L. E. Bonds, Music Director
Hasmon Abraham, electric guitar; Thomas Cupples, trumpet;
Stephen Dumaine, tuba; Matthew Guilford, trombone; Earnest
Hargrove, Hammond organ; Ralph Alan Herndon, piano & lead;
Keith Jones, trumpet; Alvin Kellibrew, electric bass; Jimmy
Russell, drums; Adel Sanchez, trumpet; Milton Stevens, trombone

11. *The Precious Blood of Jesus* 7:27 (2004)
(arr. Joseph Joubert)
Arphelius Paul Gatling, conductor
Rebecca King, soprano
The Choral Arts Society of Washington –
  Norman Scribner, Artistic Director
The Massed Choir of St. Paul's Baptist Church –
  Richmond, VA – Michelle Lightfoot, Director of Arts
  and Music
Sandtown Children of Praise – Baltimore, MD –
  Alvin E. Richardson, Jr., Music Director
Johnny Long, electric bass; Jonathan Storrs, drums;
Anthony Walker, piano

12. **He Has the Power** 4:18 (2003)
   (Leon Roberts)
   Arphelius Paul Gatling, conductor
   Joyce Ellison, mezzo-soprano
   Performing Artists Under the Lord –
      Arphelius Paul Gatling, Music Director
   Dion Clay, drums; Ralph Alan Herndon, piano;
   Christopher Suggs, electric bass

13. **I Wanna Be Ready** 3:00 (1990)
   (arr. James Miller)
   Dr. J. Weldon Norris, conductor
   Sonja Teal, soprano
   The Howard University Choir –
      Dr. J. Weldon Norris, Music Director

14. **Rock-a My Soul** 3:29 (2006)
   (arr. H. Roberts)
   Samuel L. E. Bonds, conductor
   Amon Alexander, tenor
   The Choral Arts Society of Washington –
      Norman Scribner, Artistic Director
   The Martin Luther King Tribute Choir* –
      Linda Edge Gatling, Music Director
   The Suitland High School Visual and Performing Arts
      Chamber Choir – Kenneth Boucher, Music Director
   Earnest Hargrove, pipe organ; Ralph Alan Herndon, piano;
   Alvin Kellibrew, electric bass; Jimmy Russell, drums;
   Anthony Walker, Hammond organ

15. **Wondrous Love** 4:15 (2000)
   (arr. Alice Parker and Robert Shaw)
   Arphelius Paul Gatling, conductor
   The Choral Arts Society of Washington –
      Norman Scribner, Artistic Director

16. **Glory** 3:51 (1998)
   (Traditional)
   Janice Chandler Eteme, soprano

17. **Precious Lord, Take My Hand** 6:36 (1997)
   (Thomas A. Dorsey)
   Arphelius Paul Gatling, conductor
   The Choral Arts Society of Washington –
      Norman Scribner, Artistic Director
   The Eleanor Roosevelt High School Chamber and
      Women's Choirs – Dr. Barbara Baker, Music Director
   The Young Adult Fellowship Ensemble of Metropolitan
      Baptist Church – Reverend Nolan Williams, Jr. and
      Richard Smallwood, Co-Music Directors
   Ralph Alan Herndon, piano; William Neil, pipe organ;
   Washington Symphonic Brass

Total Track Timing: **74:42**

* **The Martin Luther King Tribute Choirs were
   composed of singers from:**
Alfred Street Baptist Church – Alexandria, VA
   (2005, 2006 & 2007)
Dupont Park Seventh Day Adventist Church –
   Washington, DC (2005, 2006 & 2007)
Hope Christian Church – Lanham, MD (2007)
Metropolitan African Methodist Episcopal Church –
   Washington, DC (2005 & 2006)
Peace Lutheran Church – Washington, DC (2007)
Performing Artists Under the Lord – Washington, DC
   (2005, 2006 & 2007)
Plymouth Congregational United Church of Christ –
   Washington, DC (2005, 2006 & 2007)
Andrew Rankin Memorial Chapel,
   Howard University – Washington, DC
   (2005, 2006 & 2007)
Sargent Memorial United Presbyterian Church –
   Washington, DC (2006)
Shiloh Baptist Church – Washington, DC (2005)
Turner Memorial African Methodist Episcopal Church –
   West Hyattsville, MD (2007)

SOCIETY OF WASHINGTON
Norman Scribner, Artistic Director
Debra L. Kraft, Executive Director

CREDITS

Producers: Joseph Holt and Norman Scribner
Associate Producer: Jeffery Hart
Recording Engineers: Charles Lawson, Bruce Cain,
   Craig Lauinger and William DC Valentine
Editing & Mixing Engineers: Robert Kraft
   (Terraplane Location Recording) and Blanton Alspaugh
Tribute History Text: Jan Childress

Served as Co-Music Directors with Norman Scribner:
   Dr. J. Weldon Norris, Arphelius Paul Gatling,
   Dr. Barbara Baker and Linda Edge Gatling

Performance and text copyright © 2007,
   The Choral Arts Society of Washington

The Choral Arts Society of Washington
5225 Wisconsin Avenue, NW, Suite 603
Washington, DC 20015-2016
(p) 202.244.3669 • (f) 202.244.4244
www.choralarts.org

THE HISTORY OF THE ANNUAL CHORAL TRIBUTE
TO DR. MARTIN LUTHER KING, JR.

On the last Sunday of his life, Dr. Martin Luther King, Jr., came to the nation's capital and spoke about the changes sweeping across America. To those who knew him best, the message was familiar. Since the days of the Montgomery Bus Boycott, King had defined the African-American struggle for equal Civil Rights as "America's third revolution," one that was necessary to bring its disenfranchised black citizenry into the democratic fold. "Yes, we are in the midst of revolution," he told the congregation at Washington National Cathedral, "but our struggle must be tempered by love." The goal, he explained, was the creation of a "beloved community," where brotherhood was extended to all.

The exhilarating rise and fall of his resonant voice served to balance the message: urgent calls to action, predictions of difficult days ahead, and assurances of victory. "We shall overcome because the arc of a moral universe is long, but it bends toward justice. With this faith," he promised, "we will be able to transform the jangling discords of our nation into a beautiful symphony of brotherhood."

Four days later, the great voice was stilled forever. As riots broke out in cities across America, many wondered if King's dream of a "beautiful symphony of brotherhood" could ever be heard above the "jangling discords" of rage and retaliation. No city was hit harder by the furious rampages than Washington, DC. Within hours of King's death, large sections of the capital were in flames.

But while smoke still lingered over charred neighborhoods, a group of the city's leaders was already moving toward reconciliation by planning a memorial concert for the first anniversary of Dr. King's assassination. "We realized that we had to say something through our art that would have meaning to the community," recalls Norman Scribner, Founder and Artistic Director of The Choral Arts Society of Washington.

A year later the Choral Arts Society took part in a memorial program where musicians and civic leaders of all races honored Dr. King's memory and publicly recommitted themselves to his goal of brotherhood. These concerts continued for several years, giving voice to the timeless message of Dr. King's legacy.

In 1989, after the national holiday in King's honor had been established, the Choral Arts Society reinstated these memorial concerts as the Annual Choral Tribute to Dr. Martin Luther King, Jr. Since then, many of Washington's finest musical organizations have joined them in the Concert Hall of the John F. Kennedy Center for the Performing Arts to celebrate Martin Luther King, Jr. Day in January, close to the anniversary of his birth.

Dr. King's crusade was founded on the principles of nonviolent resistance to the injustices of segregation and the restructuring of society into one that would offer equal opportunities to all citizens – a "beloved community." These tenets guided his life's work and run like an unbroken thread through his sermons, speeches, and published works. From his words, the Annual Choral Tribute draws its themes, presented in the context of song and dance.

Performers of all races, creeds and ages are invited to perform at the Annual Choral Tribute and a representative sampling of their music appears on the enclosed CD. The music, too, is purposefully eclectic, acknowledging not only Dr. King's wide-ranging musical tastes but the Tribute's heartfelt commitment to re-create through art the beloved community – the beautiful symphony of brotherhood – that he promised would one day be ours.

The Choral Arts Society of Washington (CASW), led by Founder and Artistic Director Norman Scribner, is celebrating its forty-third season in 2007-2008. The ensemble is recognized internationally as one of the major symphonic choruses in the nation, and it is a moving force in Washington, DC's cultural scene. CASW has presented an annual subscription series in the John F. Kennedy Center for the Performing Arts Concert Hall since it opened in the fall of 1971. The Choral Arts Society presents additional concerts throughout the metropolitan area, including the Annual Choral Tribute to Dr. Martin Luther King, Jr. – a multicultural community outreach performance. CASW also engages in numerous educational activities including the ground-breaking arts*ACCESS* program – a partnership between the Choral Arts Society and DC Public Schools, serving grades one through six and employing the creative and participatory nature of the arts to teach reading, mathematics, science, and social studies. In addition to frequent performances with the National Symphony Orchestra, CASW has appeared with the orchestras of Atlanta, Baltimore, BBC, Cincinnati and Cleveland, as well as the New York, Czech, and Israel Philharmonics; and under the batons of such notable conductors as Leonard Bernstein, James Conlon, Antal Dorati, Erich Kunzel, Erich Leinsdorf, Lorin Maazel, Helmuth Rilling, Mstislav Rostropovich, Julius Rudel, Leonard Slatkin, Robert Shaw, and Yuri Temirkanov.

CASW has appeared at the Proms Festival, the Spoleto Music Festival, the Evian Festival and the Grand Teton Music Festival. The Choral Arts Society traveled with Rostropovich and the National Symphony Orchestra to Moscow in 1993 to join forces for an historic performance in Red Square to an audience of over 100,000. CASW has appeared in many televised performances including *A Capitol Fourth* – broadcast live from the National Mall, and CBS Television's *The Kennedy Center Honors*. Recordings include *Of Rage and Remembrance* by John Corigliano with the National Symphony Orchestra; *Make Me Drunk With Your Kisses* featuring Alexander Knaifel's *Chapter Eight,* with cellist Mstislav Rostropovich; *Ein Deutsches Requiem* by Johannes Brahms; *Symphony No. 13 (Babi Yar)* by Dmitri Shostakovich, and *Vespers* by Sergei Rachmaninoff. Releases on the Naxos label include *Yizkor Requiem* by Thomas Beveridge, *A Choral Tribute to Dr. Martin Luther King, Jr. – The First Ten Years, There Shall A Star – Choral Jewels for Christmas* and *Celebrating Sacred Rhythms* (2006 Washington Area Music Award winner for Best Classical Recording).

Precious Lord, Take My Hand

Precious Lord, take my hand,
Lead me on, let me stand,
I am tired, I am weak, I am worn;
Through the storm, through the night,
Lead me on to the light:

Take my hand, precious Lord,
Lead me home.

When my way grows drear,
Precious Lord, linger near,
When my life is almost gone,
Hear my cry, hear my call,
Hold my hand lest I fall:

Take my hand, precious Lord,
Lead me home.

—Thomas A. Dorsey
(Adapted from music by George N. Allen)